Elegant
COTTON • WOOL • SILK
QUILTS

Rami Kim

American Quilter's Society
P. O. Box 3290 • Paducah, KY 42002-3290
www.AmericanQuilter.com

M000287999

Located in Paducah, Kentucky, the American Quilter's Society (AQS) is dedicated to promoting the accomplishments of today's quilters. Through its publications and events, AQS strives to honor today's quiltmakers and their work and to inspire future creativity and innovation in quiltmaking.

EXECUTIVE BOOK EDITOR: ANDI MILAM REYNOLDS
SENIOR BOOK EDITOR: LINDA BAXTER LASCO
GRAPHIC DESIGN: ELAINE WILSON
COVER DESIGN: MICHAEL BUCKINGHAM
FASHION PHOTOGRAPHY: WOOIL KIM
QUILT PHOTOGRAPHY: CHARLES R. LYNCH

ATTENTION PHOTOCOPYING SERVICE: Please note the following— Publisher and author give permission to print pages 15, 19, 21–25, 31–38, 52, 60, 63, and 71 for personal use only.

Additional copies of this book may be ordered from the American Quilter's Society, PO Box 3290, Paducah, KY 42002-3290, or online at www.AmericanQuilter.com.

Text © 2012, Author, Rami Kim
Artwork © 2012, American Quilter's Society

LIBRARY OF CONGRESS CATALOGING-IN-PUBLICATION DATA

Kim, Rami.
  Elegant cotton wool silk quilts / by Rami Kim.
    pages cm
  Summary: "Add Asian flair and Rami Kim's distinctive elegance to your quilts, wearables, and home dec projects. Asian art and culture provide the inspiration for six fabric projects. Learn the ancient fabric arts of chopkey (folding), bojahgey (piecing) and weaving. Projects are worked in cotton, wool, or silk, the fibers reflecting Eastern and Western reverence for all things natural"--Provided by publisher.
  ISBN 978-1-60460-024-7
  1. Patchwork--Patterns. 2. Quilting--Patterns. I. Title.
  TT835.K488658 2012
  746.46--dc23
                        2012039251

TITLE PAGE: **PENNY RUGS – wool quilt, detail. Full quilt on page 16.**

OPPOSITE: **CUBES AND FLOWERS – silk quilt, detail. Full quilt on page 56.**

Acknowledgments

Very special thanks to:

My editor, Linda Lasco, and all the publishing staff at AQS for their help and advice again.

Hobbs Bonded Fibers, for supplying the best battings for my works.

My husband, Ken Lee, for constant love and friendship.

My two precious daughters, Deanna and Chelsey, for letting me know what the joy of being a mom is.

My parents and parents-in-law, for their unconditional love and support.

Phyllis and the ladies at the Thistle Dew Quilt Shop for being my biggest fans.

Susan, for relentlessly pushing me to achieve perfection.

"Stitching with Love," my church quilting group, for showing me the best way to serve God and community.

Dedication

To God who graciously gave us this beautiful & fascinating world. Wish everyone could see it through his or her own eyes, not through someone else's.

Contents

OPPOSITE: **SUNSET OVER A LOTUS POND I – wool quilt, detail. Full quilt on page 26.**

Preface

Elegant designs with Asian flair demonstrate the breadth of Asian culture. The designs here put special emphasis on the ancient cultures of Korea.

Each chapter focuses on a specific element of the culture and shows how Asian concepts can be translated and incorporated into contemporary crafts.

This book will serve as an introduction to and a window into the "Land of Morning Calm." It also documents the many millennia of rich cultural development on the Korean peninsula and demonstrates how this evolution contributes to today's global society. Because of the diverse climate, cotton, silk, and other fabrics were present during phases of this cultural development.

Some designs trace their origins back to the period of the three kingdoms (Koguryo, Baekche, and Shilla), which spanned the years from 100 BC to 667 AD. No design was executed only in a single fabric. The creativity ran the gamut of fabrics available to artisans.

The current craze for Asian fabrics demonstrates that needle artists everywhere are eager to adopt something that feels different and new.

Though many of the designs are actually more than a few thousand years old, this will be the first glimpse through the eyes of the Western viewer.

Designs from Architecture

As in many other countries, details from Korean architectural designs found in historic places can provide sources of inspiration for modern day quilters.

Brick walls of ancient castle tiles, traditional paper-backed lattice windows, ceramic roof tiles, and some decorative paintings called Dahn-Chung found on temples and palaces suggest distinguished colors and designs for Western quilters.

I designed three quilts inspired by castle tiles and roof tiles and combined with very American Log Cabin blocks and Penny Rug designs, creating exotic harmony between East and West.

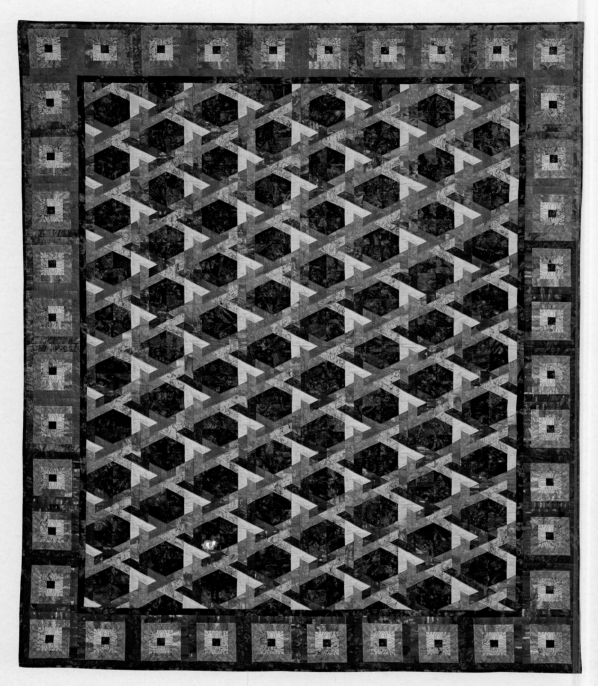

Project 1

INTERLOCKING CASTLE TILES – COTTON QUILT

76" x 90¾", made by the author

Inspired by ancient castle wall tiles, this strongly geometric pattern fits beautifully into the modern quilting art. A traditional American Log Cabin border contains the tiles and provides the perfect finishing touch.

Project 1
INTERLOCKING CASTLE TILES – COTTON QUILT

Inspired by ancient castle wall tiles, this strongly geometric pattern fits beautifully into the modern quilting art. A traditional American Log Cabin border contains the tiles and provides the perfect finishing touch.

Yardage Requirements

+ 3 yards dark brown batik cotton background
+ 1¾ yards EACH yellow, orange, yellow green, and light blue batik cottons
+ 2½ yards EACH fuchsia and purple batik cottons
+ 7½ yards backing fabric (seamed crosswise; more needed for directional fabric)
+ 83" x 98" batting
+ ¾ yard binding

Cutting Instructions

+ Make 84 tile blocks and 40 Log Cabin blocks.
+ Use the pattern templates on page 15 to cut out the pieces.

+ With yellow 1¾" strips—cut 84 of A, C, D, E
+ With orange 1¾" strips—cut 84 of B, C', E
+ With fuchsia 1¾" strips—cut 84 of C, C', E, F
+ With yellow green 1¾" strips—cut 84 of C, C', E, F
+ With light blue 1¾" strips—cut 84 of B, C', E
+ With purple 1¾" strips—cut 84 of A, C, D, E
+ With dark brown 3" strips—cut 168 of G and 168 of G'

+ For the Log Cabin border blocks (see photo page 14) cut 1⅝" strips of yellow, orange, fuchsia, yellow green, light blue, and purple and 1⅝" x 1⅝" squares of dark brown to make 40 Log Cabin blocks.

+ For the inner border cut 7 dark brown 1½" strips.

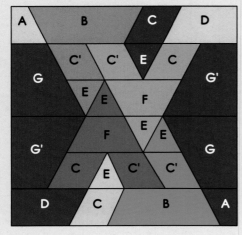

Make 84 tile blocks

Sewing Instructions

Following the diagram provided for colors and shapes, stitch the units as listed below.

Sew half a block:
    Unit 1—A + B + C + D
    Unit 2—C' + C' + E + C
    Unit 3—E + E + F
    Unit 4—Unit 2 + Unit 3
    Unit 5—G + Unit 4 + G'
    Unit 6—Unit 1 + Unit 5

Repeat these 6 units with the colors indicated to make the other half of a block.

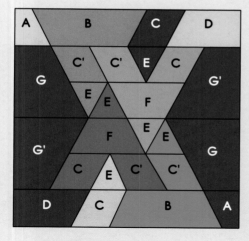

Color placement

Stitch two half-block units together to make a whole block. Make 84 blocks.

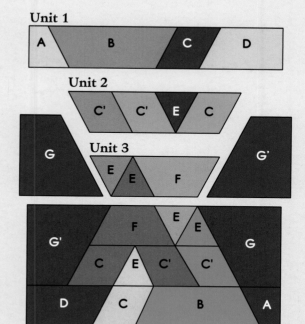

Block assembly – make 84.

Connect 10 blocks in a row, matching the seams. Make 4 rows of 10 blocks.

Make 4 rows of 10 blocks each.

Connect 11 blocks in a row, matching the
seams. Make 4 rows of 11 blocks.

Make 4 rows of 11 blocks each.

Stitch row to row, alternating the 10 block set
and 11 block sets, offsetting by half of a block
as shown, and matching the seams to create the
look of an interlocking tile design.

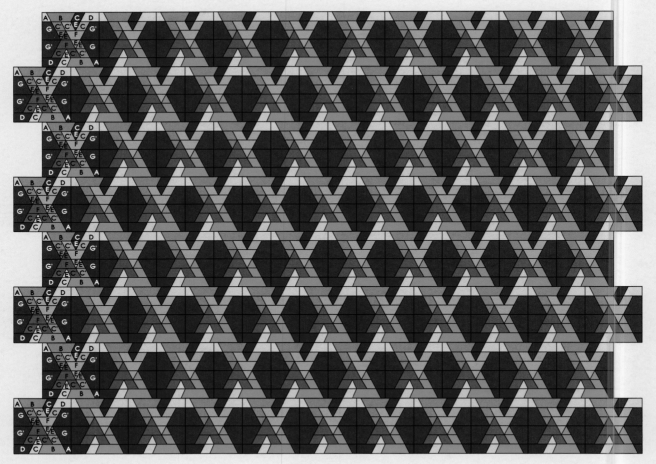

Offset the rows.

Square the stitched top to measure 59½" x 74¼", trimming the excess from the 11-block rows.

59½"

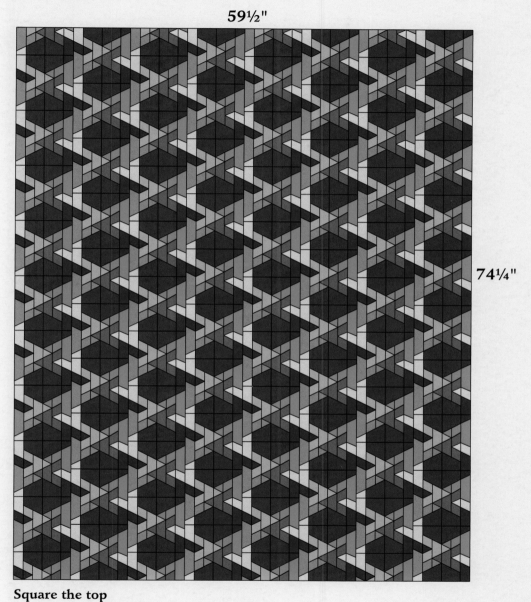

74¼"

Square the top

Join the dark brown inner border strips as needed to make the border strips:

- 2 strips 1½" x 61½"
- 2 strips of 1½" x 74¼"

Stitch the inner border strips to the squared interlocking tile center following the diagram on page 14.

Stitch Log Cabin block borders as shown to finish the quilt top.

> **Design Option:** You can adjust sizes of the quilt as you wish. Make Log Cabin border blocks first to your desired size and adjust the center interlocking tile part and inner border strips to fit the borders.

Quilt with your favorite pattern.

Prepare about 350" of 2½" strips for double-fold binding.

Log Cabin block (square block to 7¾" x 7¾")

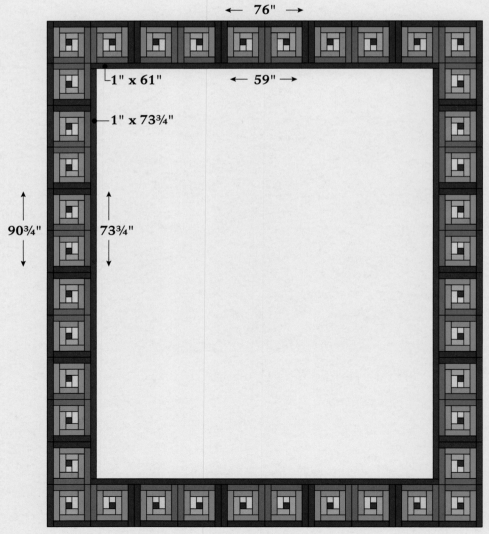

← 76" →

1" x 61"   ← 59" →

1" x 73¾"

90¾"   73¾"

Log Cabin border

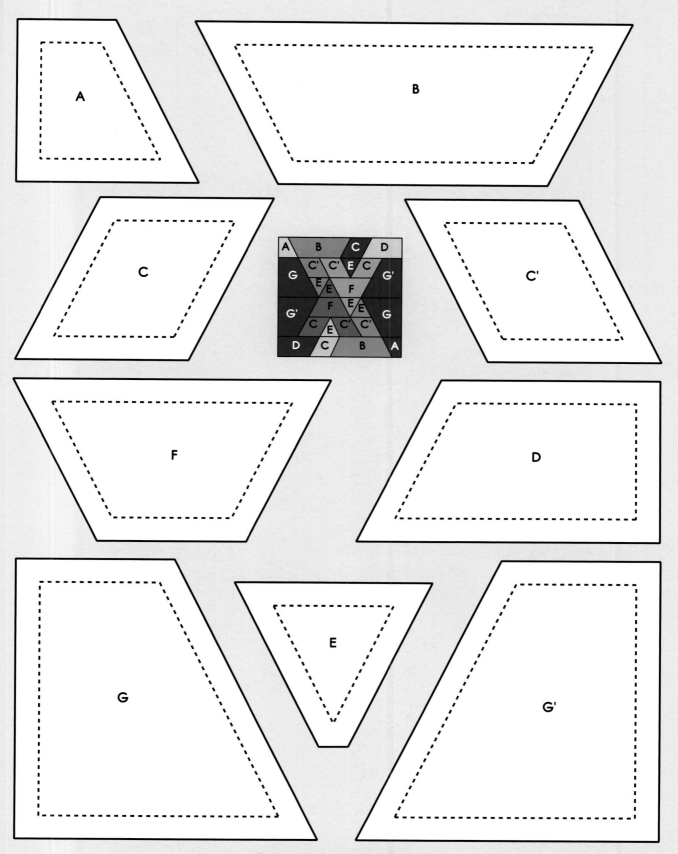

Patterns shown at 100%.

Project 2
PENNY RUGS – WOOL QUILT

PENNY RUGS with designs from Korean roof tiles, 31" x 42",
wool quilt made by the author

American Penny Rugs became popular in the late 1800s as decorative accents for tables and beds with their warm, whimsical appeal. Penny Rugs earned their name during the Civil War era, using copper penny coins as templates to cut the wool scraps and felt circles that formed the basis of the works. The term "rug" means something that covers or lies on top, so they were not meant to use on the floor as one might think.

Project 2
PENNY RUGS – WOOL QUILT

American Penny Rugs became popular in the late 1800s as decorative accents for tables and beds with their warm, whimsical appeal. Penny Rugs earned their name during the Civil War era, using copper penny coins as templates to cut the wool scraps and felt circles that formed the basis of the works. The term "rug" means something that covers or lies on top, so they were not meant to use on the floor as one might think.

Most of the Penny Rugs were embellished with simple shapes like leaves, flowers, animals, and other natural motifs, appliquéd with blanket stitches.

I researched designs in Korean roof tiles and found shapes that could be exotically wonderful on variations of Penny Rugs. Asian interpretations of flowers, leaves, clouds, and mountains beautifully adorn this wool Penny Rug quilt.

Yardage Requirements

- 1¼ yards background wool flannel
- ¼ yard EACH felted wool and wool felt in pale yellow, yellow gold, orange, brick red, yellow green, pale pink, pale blue, purple, violet, and blue
- ⅛ yard wool plaid for small circles in pennies
- Embroidery floss in matching colors to wool felt and felted wool
- 1¼ yards backing
- 1¼ yards batting*

*I used Hobbs Thermore batting, which provided the perfect thickness for this wool quilt.

I recycled my old wool flannel skirt for the background rectangles. I also I felted two of my old jackets to make the pennies in this quilt. I simply washed jackets in washer with hot water and dried several times with hot-cycle dryer. Boil some water and add it to the washer for a better felting result!

Sewing Instructions

Print the patterns from pages 21–25. For background rectangles a ¼" seam allowance is included.

Cut the background rectangles as shown.

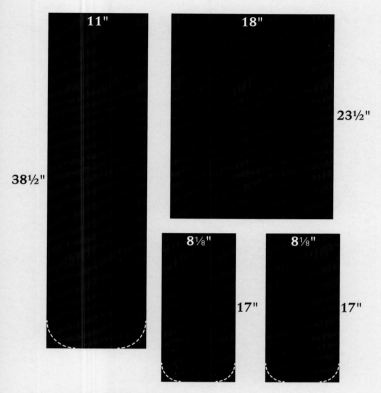

Background rectangles

Cut 58 large circles with dark brown wool and 29 small circles with plaid wool using the patterns provided below.

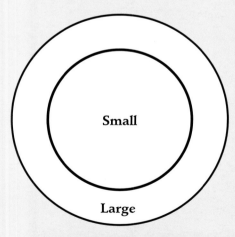

Cut 58 large and 29 small circles.

Pin one small plaid circle to the center of one large dark brown circle. With two strands of embroidery floss in yellow-gold, blanket stitch a small circle to a large circle around the raw edge. Repeat to make a total of 29 layered circles. Matching raw edges, pin one large dark brown circle to the back of one layered circle (layered side up).

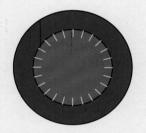

Make 29 layered circles.

Using two strands of embroidery floss in dark brown, blanket stitch the large circles together to finish the penny. Repeat to make a total of 29 pennies.

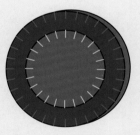

Add third circle to complete each penny.

Refer to the quilt design and motif patterns (pages 21–25). Trace the motifs onto template material and use them to cut out felted wool and wool felt in matching colors. Blanket stitch the motifs to the backgrounds with two strands of embroidery floss in matching colors.

Press with a pressing cloth to set the stitches. Cut out backing of the same shape as all four pieces.

To finish each piece, place the appliquéd top and backing, right sides together, on a piece of batting, cut to size, and using a ¼" seam allowance stitch through all three layers around all sides, leaving an opening. Trim off corners to reduce bulkiness. Turn right-side out through the opening. Slipstitch the openings closed. Press.

Make 3 sets of pennies for connecting the panels—one with 16 pennies, one with 7, and one with 6. Following the diagram below, connect the four appliquéd finished background panels by tacking pennies to the sides of the panels.

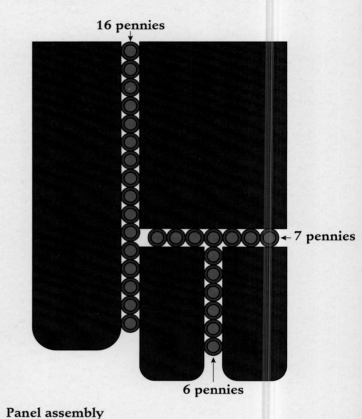

Panel assembly

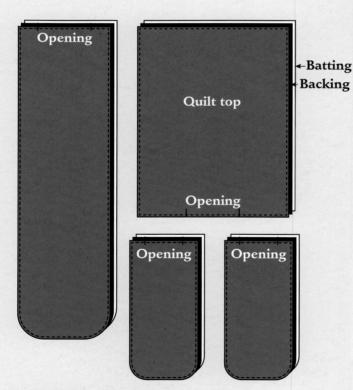

Finishing the panels

Use 3 strands of embroidery floss to echo-quilt around the appliquéd motifs through all thicknesses with ¼" running stitches.

Design Option: You can create the same design quilt with cotton fabrics using hand appliqué stitches or machine blanket stitches.

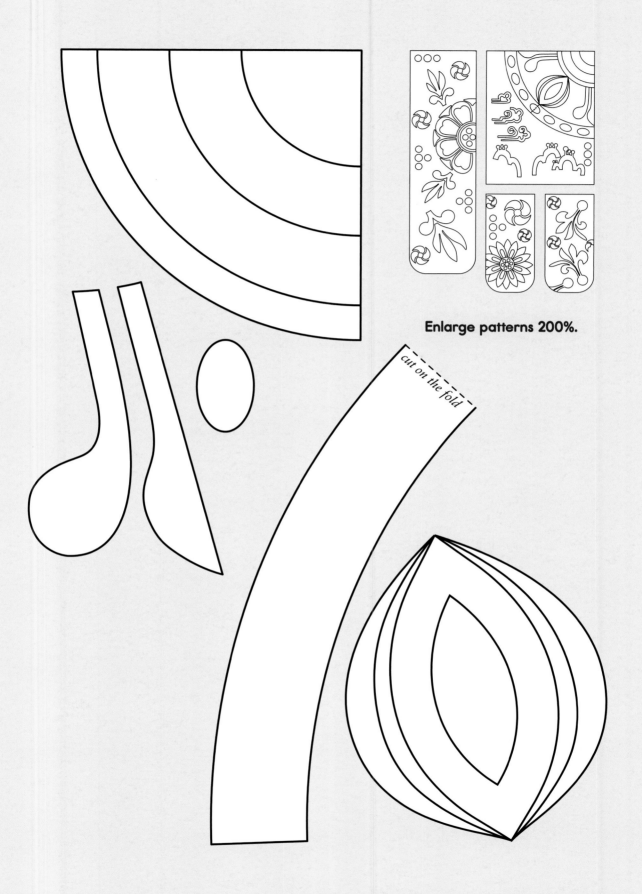

Enlarge patterns 200%.

cut on the fold

Enlarge patterns 200%.

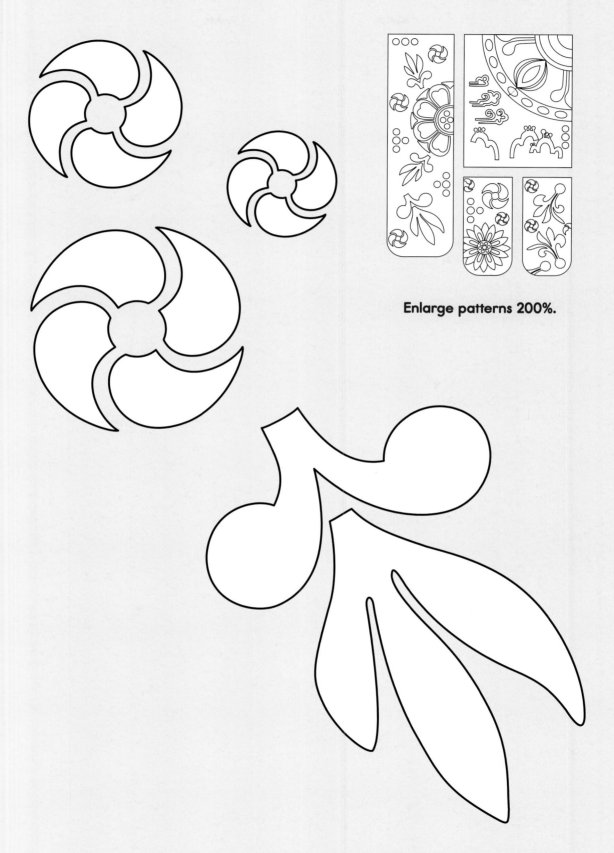

Enlarge patterns 200%.

Enlarge patterns 200%.

Enlarge patterns 200%.

Project 3
SUNSET OVER A LOTUS POND I
THREE-PANEL WOOL QUILT

PENNY RUGS with designs from Korean roof tiles, 31" x 42",
wool quilt made by the author

Designs such as sun, mountain, water, rock, and cloud represent longevity in Asia because these objects exist eternally in nature. Lotus blossoms symbolize spiritual purity and freedom from the worries of a secular world.

Project 3

SUNSET OVER A LOTUS POND I

THREE-PANEL WOOL QUILT

Designs such as sun, mountain, water, rock, and cloud represent longevity in Asia because these objects exist eternally in nature. Lotus blossoms symbolize spiritual purity and freedom from the worries of a secular world.

In this three-panel wool quilt with pennies, all these elements are harmonized through Asian-influenced colors.

Yardage Requirements

- 1¼ yards purple wool flannel for the background and small pennies
- ¼ yard or fat quarter EACH felted wool and wool felt in assorted colors—blues, greens, pinks, yellows, reds, and purples
- ¼ yard baby pink wool flannel for the large pennies
- embroidery floss in matching colors
- 1 yard cotton backing
- 1 yard Hobbs Thermore batting

Sewing Instructions

Print the patterns from pages 31–38.

Cut 1 rectangle and 2 circles from the background wool flannel, backing, and batting using the patterns provided. A ½" seam allowance is included.

Trace design motifs with tracing paper or freezer paper adding ¼" seam allowance only to sections that will be placed under other motifs. Cut out wool felt or felted wool following colors in the sample quilt.

Place and baste design motifs onto the background wool flannel using hand-basting stitches or fabric glue.

Appliqué motifs using blanket stitches with double stranded embroidery floss in matching colors.

Make 16 elongated penny units.

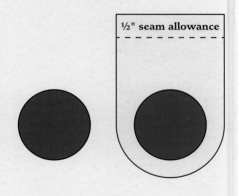

½" seam allowance

Cut 32 elongated back pieces of pink wool flannel.

Cut 16 circular pennies of purple wool flannel.

Appliqué one purple penny onto one pink elongated back piece using blanket stitches. (It takes a 25" long double strand of embroidery floss for each appliqué.)

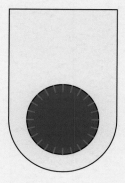

Add another pink elongated back piece to the back and stitch the two pink back pieces together around the edges using blanket stitches. (It takes a 38" long double strand of embroidery floss for each unit.)

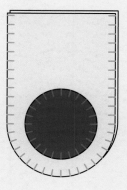

Make 48 circular penny units using patterns provided on pages 31–32.

Cut 96 large circles of pink wool flannel.

Cut 48 small circles of purple wool flannel.

Appliqué 48 small purple circles onto 48 large pink circles using blanket stitches. (It takes a 25" long double strand of embroidery floss for each appliqué.)

Add a large pink circle to the back and stitch the two large pink circles together using blanket stitches. (It takes a 36" long double strand of embroidery floss for each unit.)

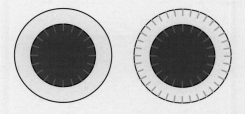

For the center rectangular panel, baste 8 elongated penny units to the top edge of the background and another 8 elongated penny units to the bottom edge with right sides together (circular penny side down), basting ¼" from the edges.

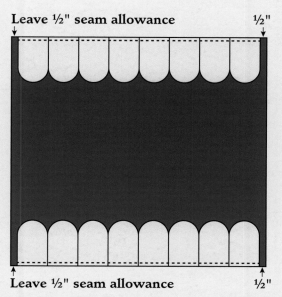

Leave ½" seam allowance   **½"**

Leave ½" seam allowance   **½"**

Baste elongated pennies ¼" from the raw edge of the background.

Place the quilt top and backing right sides together. Add one layer of batting to the wrong side of the backing.

Stitch all three layers together using a ½" seam allowance, leaving an 8" opening on one side for turning later. Grade the seam allowances to reduce bulkiness.

Turn right-side out. Slipstitch the opening closed and press.

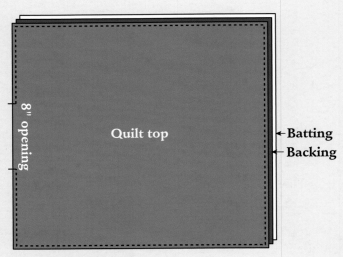

Finishing the panel

For the circular panels, place the quilt top and backing right sides together. Add one layer of batting to the wrong side of the backing.

Stitch all three layers together using a ½" seam allowance, leaving a 5" opening to turn later.

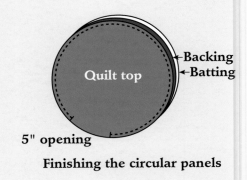

Finishing the circular panels

Grade the seam allowances.

Turn right-side out. Slipstitch the opening closed and press.

Hand stitch 24 penny units around the finished edge of each circular panel.

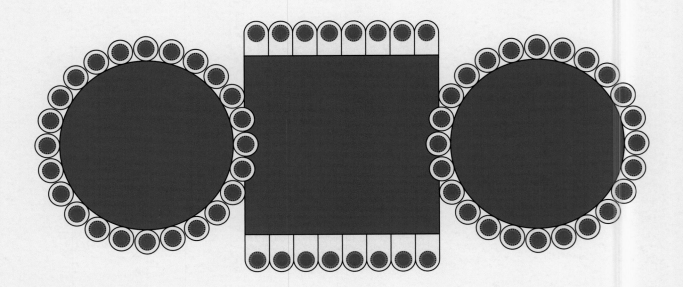

Enlarge patterns 200%.

½" seam allowance

Elongated penny

Enlarge pattern 200%.

Small

Large

Full-size

Enlarge pattern 200%.

Enlarge pattern 200%.

Enlarge pattern 200%.

Enlarge pattern 200%.

Enlarge pattern 200%.

Enlarge pattern 200%.

Architecture Gallery

SUNSET OVER A LOTUS POND II

38" x 28" embroidered and appliquéd silk wallhanging, made by the author

SUNSET POND, art-to-wear coat, made and modeled by the author

WOOL VEST, art-to-wear, made by the author

Chopkey
Korean Folding Techniques

I introduced Chopkey, a Korean form of paper folding, in my first book, *Folded Fabric Elegance* (AQS, 2007). Here again I use fabrics instead of paper to create a three-dimensional quilt wallhanging.

Chopkey traces its origin back about 1500 years. I learned Chopkey at an early age from my mother and grandmother, just like any other Korean kid. It still fascinates me to transform two-dimensional materials into unexpected three-dimensional shapes.

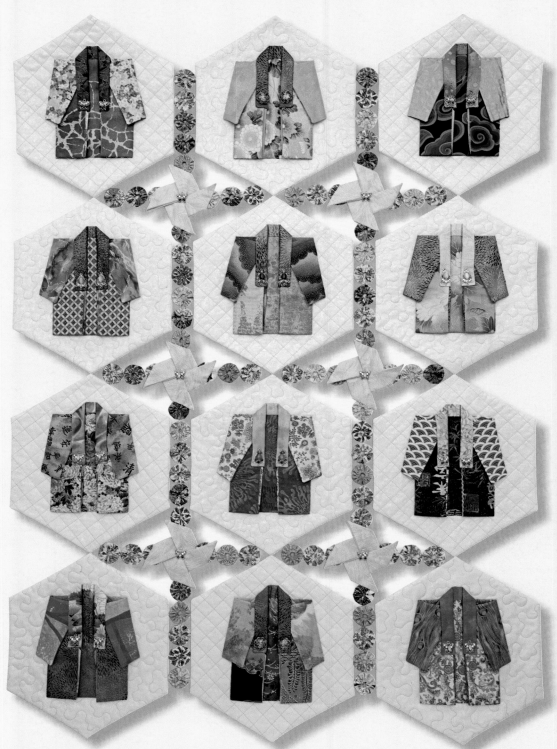

Project 4
Doo-Roo-Mah-Gey – cotton quilt

31" x 43", 3-D Korean coat, cotton wallhanging, made by the author

Project 4
DOO-ROO-MAH-GEY – COTTON QUILT

Doo-Roo-Mah-Gey is a name for a coat of Korean traditional costumes called Hanbok. This quilted wallhanging is fat-quarter friendly and expandable or reducible to any size you wish, depending on how many hexagon blocks are included. When you are comfortable with this folding technique, try it with silk dupioni.

Yardage Requirements for 12 Blocks

❖ 1½ yards background ivory cotton
❖ 20-30 fat quarters in assorted colors
❖ 1½ yards Hobbs fusible batting
❖ 1½ yards ivory cotton backing
❖ Charms for embellishment

Making Background Hexagon Blocks

1. Cut twelve 13" x 13" squares of ivory background fabric and batting. Add batting to the wrong side of the fabric squares and fuse the batting.

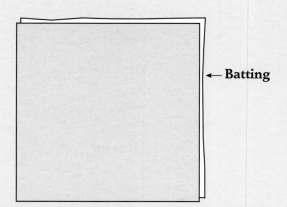

← **Batting**

Layering the background fabric and batting

2. Quilt the two layers together with gold-colored rayon thread. I used a 1" diagonal grid on six squares and free-motion stippling on the other six.

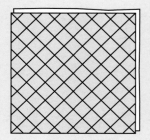

Quilt 6 with a grid and 6 with stippling.

3. Use the hexagon pattern provided (page 52) and trim off the excess.

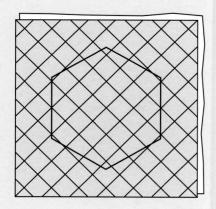

Folding 3-D Korean Doo-Roo-Mah-Gey Coat

1. You need three coordinating or contrasting colored fabrics for one coat.

- ✤ Cut one 16" x 9" rectangle for the body (a small print fabric works well).
- ✤ Cut one 16" x 9" rectangle for the sleeves (second fabric).
- ✤ Cut two 2" x 9" rectangles for the collar (third fabric).

2. Stitch a collar piece to the short end of both rectangles, right sides together, with a ¼" seam allowance, matching the raw edges. Press the seams toward the collar pieces.

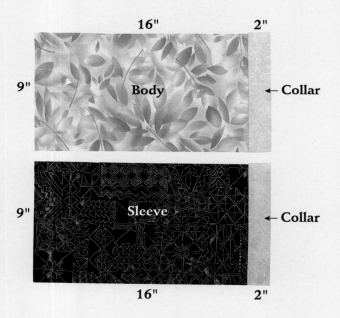

3. With right sides together, stitch the body and sleeve rectangles together, aligning the collar sections. Leave a 2" opening as shown. Trim corners and turn right-side out. Press. You do not have to close the opening since it will be hidden on the back.

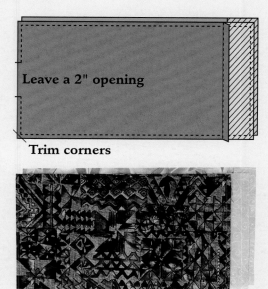

4. With the body side facing up, fold half the collar piece toward the back sleeve side and steam press.

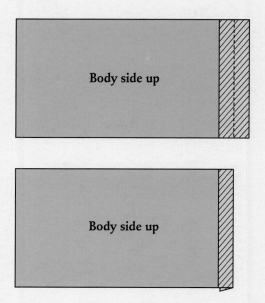

5. Lightly press a center crease.

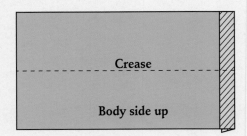

6. Fold the collar part toward body as shown and steam press.

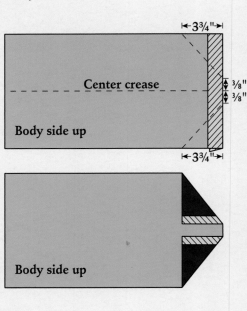

7. Fold the bottom edge up 3½" and steam press.

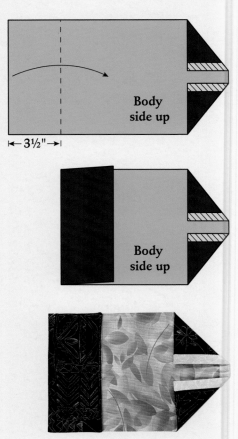

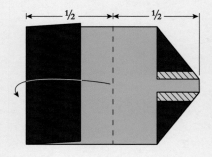

8. Fold back the folded portion toward the sleeve side.

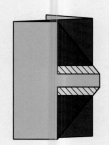

9. Lightly press creases between the folded collar edges and sleeve edges.

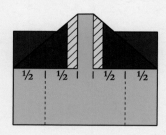

10. Place both sleeve edges under the collar.

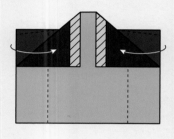 

11. Pull down the sleeves ¼" and steam press.

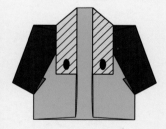

12. Stitch two charms on the collar.

13. Center the 3-D coat on a hexagon background block and slipstitch in place.

Finishing the Blocks

1. Use the pattern to cut 12 hexagons of ivory backing fabric.

2. With right sides together, use a ¼" seam allowance to stitch a backing hexagon to a quilted hexagon with a 3-D coat, leaving a 3" opening.

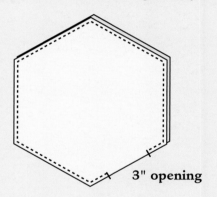

3" opening

3. Trim the corners and turn right-side out. Slipstitch to close the opening. Make 12 blocks.

Making Yo-Yos to Connect the Hexagon Blocks

1. Using the circle template page 52 to cut out 80 circles 2⅝" in diameter using assorted colors.

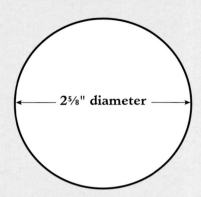

Cut 2⅝" diameter circles.

2. With the wrong side up, fold down a ³⁄₁₆" seam allowance. Use two strands of cotton thread to make ⅛" running stitches around the folded edge.

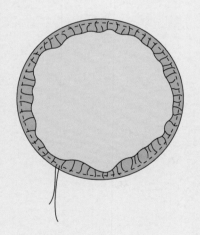

3. Pull the thread tight, make a secure knot, and hide the tail of the thread.

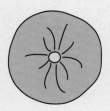

Making Folded 3-D Pinwheels to Connect the Blocks

1. Cut 12 squares 5¼" x 5¼" of tone-on-tone fabric. (You need two squares to make one folded 3-D pinwheel.)

2. Using a ¼" seam allowance, stitch two squares, right sides together, leaving a 1½" opening. Trim the corners and turn right-side out. Press.

3. Fold 3-D pinwheels following diagrams a–f below and continuing on page 49.

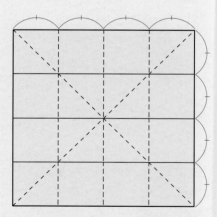

a. Make creases by pressing with steam iron as shown above.

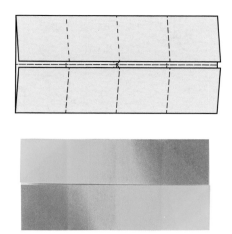

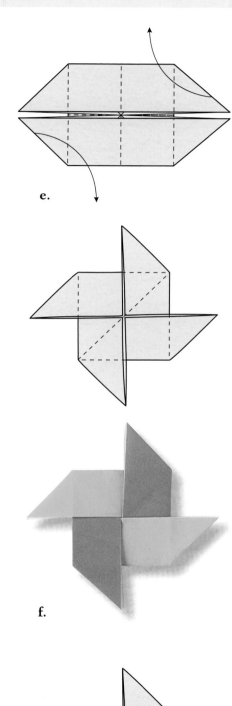

e.

b. Fold the square in half as shown along creases.

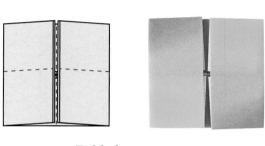

c. Fold along creases.

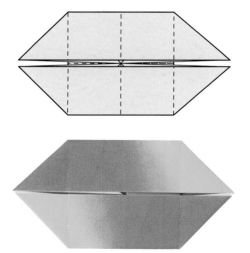

d. Pull out diagonal creases of four corners.

f.

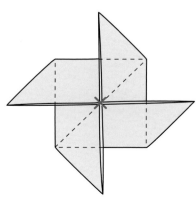

4. Add a charm to embellish.

Connecting Hexagon Blocks with Yo-Yos and Pinwheels

1. Connect 4 yo-yos in assorted colors by stitching with 2 strands of cotton thread. Hide the knots and tails of thread inside the yo-yos. Make 8 sets of 4 yo-yos each.

2. Connect 2 finished hexagon blocks using one set of 4 yo-yos as shown. Stitch the touching points together between hexagon blocks and yo-yos using 2 strands of cotton thread. Hide knots and tails of thread again.

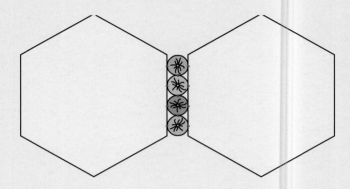

3. Connect all 12 blocks using the 8 sets of yo-yos.

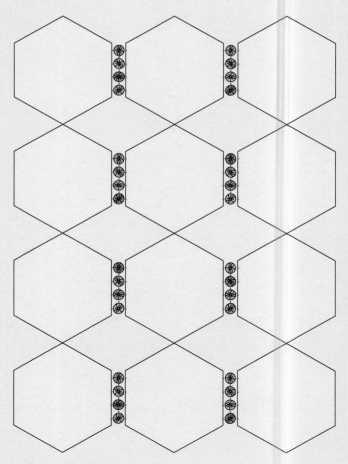

Assembly diagram

4. You need 8 yo-yos and one 3-D pinwheel for each inside opening. Arrange the yo-yos as shown. Stitch the yo-yo touching points first.

5. Position a 3-D pinwheel on top of the center yo-yos and tack in place.

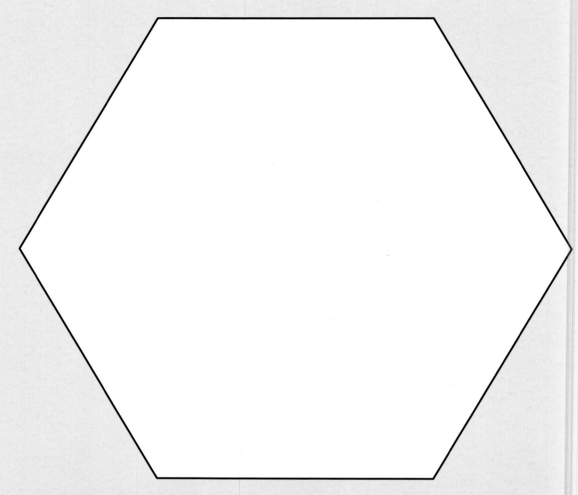

Enlarge hexagon pattern 200%.

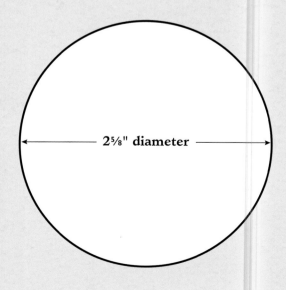

2⅝" diameter

Chopkey Gallery

I designed a pattern of Doo-Roo-Mah-Gey when I created this PEACOCK DREAM ensemble for an invitational Fairfield Fashion Show years ago. Believe it or not I fell asleep on my sewing table one night and had this wonderful dream about a peacock. This ensemble is the result from a sketch I made after that dream. Silk dupioni was the sole fabric used and free-motion machine embroidery with rayon and metallic threads and foundation piecing created the peacock feathers.

PEACOCK DREAM art-to wear emsemble, made by the author

Weaving with Folded Strips

I've been always fascinated by woven pieces like baskets, rugs, woven fabric, and nettings. The journey through the history of weaving suggests that there is evidence of cloth being made in Mesopotamia and in Turkey as far back as 7000 to 8000 BC. Weaving serves as a metaphor for life in the art, literature, and mythology of many cultures.

Project 5
CUBES AND FLOWERS – SILK QUILT

42" x 61", made by the author

Project 5

CUBES AND FLOWERS – SILK QUILT

By folding 1¼" fabric strips and weaving them in three different directions, you can form the optical illusion of cubes.

Combining various colors for warps and wefts creates even more enchanting patterns. Three-dimensional folded flowers from lined Prairie Points adorn a woven cube design to add delicate volume textures.

Yardage Requirements

Assuming 45" width fabrics, 40" usable:

- ✤ 1 yard flower motif fabric (large flower)
- ✤ ¾ yard EACH brocade silk in two different colors for sashing and border
- ✤ Silk dupioni:
    - ✤ 2 yards dark green for woven strips for the warp strips
    - ✤ 1 yard yellow green for the weft strips
    - ✤ 1 yard teal green for the weft strips
    - ✤ 1 yard purple for the weft strips
    - ✤ ½ yard orange for the weft strips
- ✤ ¼ yard EACH silk dupioni and silk organza in light purple for lined prairie points folded flowers
- ✤ 2½ yards Hobb's Thermore batting
- ✤ 1⅞ yards backing
- ✤ ½ yard binding
- ✤ 6 yards fusible interfacing
- ✤ 50–100 ¼" crystal beads

Weaving a Cube Design

Additional Supplies

- ✤ padded weaving surface
- ✤ chalk marker
- ✤ bodkin

Weaving Method

1. Cut 1¼" dark green strips (crosswise grain for cottons and lengthwise grain for silk dupioni) for the warps (the backbone of a weaving structure). Fold them in half lengthwise by bringing both edges in toward the center. Press.

2. For the base of your weaving structure, cut out your choice of lightweight fusible interfacing 1" larger than the shape you are going to weave. Position with the fusible side up.

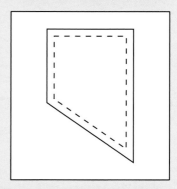

1" larger than pattern piece

3. Place the fusible on the padded surface with the fusible side up for weaving and pin both ends of the warp folded strips in vertical rows to cover the base, butting the strips closely together.

4. Draw a 30-degree angle line across the warp strips with a chalk marker.

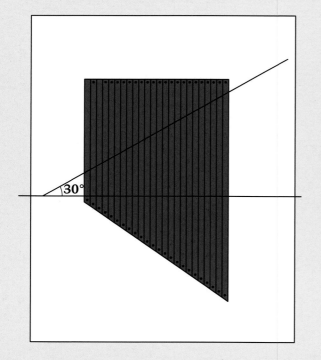

5. Cut 1¼" yellow green strips for the weft strips. Fold and press as before.

6. Weave the three-strip repeat pattern, aligning the edge of the first strip with the marked line. Use a bodkin to pull the folded strips through the warp strips. Pin both ends of each strip as you finish weaving it in place.

Weave the first strip:
 *over 1 warp strip
 under 2 warp strips*
 repeat between the *s

Weave the second strip:
 under 1
 *over 1
 under 2*
 repeat between the *s

Weave the third strip:
 under 2
 *over 1
 under 2*
 repeat between the *s

Repeat the three steps to cover the entire area of warp strips, maintaining the 30-degree angle of the strips.

7. Cut 1¼" strips of teal green, purple, and orange. Fold and press as before. Weave the weft strips as shown in the photo going in the other direction from the first set of weft strips, following the same pattern of going under 2 weft strips and over 1 weft strip, forming the tops of the cubes. Pin both ends.

Repeat with different colors of your choice.

8. When the weaving is done, fuse the woven piece to the interfacing base with a low temperature dry iron to hold the shape.

9. Remove the pins from the padded surface. Pin the strips along the edges of the fusible to hold the shape. Stitch vertical lines through the centers of the warp strips through all thicknesses using a walking foot. Give a final pressing.

10. Use the pattern piece to cut out the shape.

Folding 3-D Flowers from Lined Prairie Points

1. Cut two strips of two different widths in two different colors.

> 2 strips 1¾" x 45"—this color is shown in the center as lines.
> 2 strips 1½" x 45"—this color is shown in side triangles.

2. Stitch 2 strips using a ¼" seam allowance, right sides together.

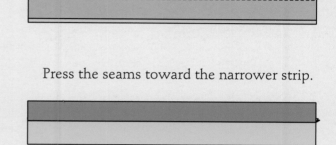

Press the seams toward the narrower strip.

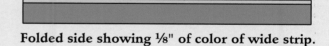

Fold the strip-set in half lengthwise, wrong sides together, and press.

Folded side showing ⅛" of color of wide strip.

With the wider strip facing you, fold Prairie Point units, cutting off each one as it is folded.

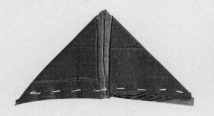

3. Make running stitches ⅛" from the raw edge through all thicknesses to gather the Prairie Point into the shape of a flower petal.

4. Connect 5 petals to make one blossom.

5. Make a yo-yo using a 2¼" in diameter circle and tack it to the center of a blossom.

Making the Silk Wallhanging

1. Cut fabrics as indicated in the cutting diagram, page 61.

2. Make the 4 woven cubes sections following the Weaving Instructions (pages 57–59).

3. Stitch the 3 flower motif sections to the brocade sashings. Press the seams open.

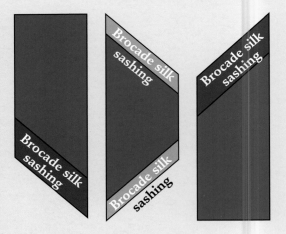

4. To adjust the thickness of the 3 sashed flower sections to the thickness of the woven pieces, underline them with a layer of Hobb's Thermore batting, which is a very thin polyester batting perfect for this purpose. Spray or hand baste to the wrong sides of sashed flower sections.

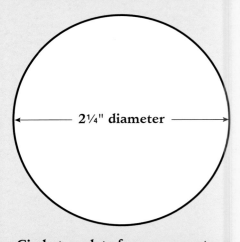

2¼" **diameter**

Circle template for yo-yo centers

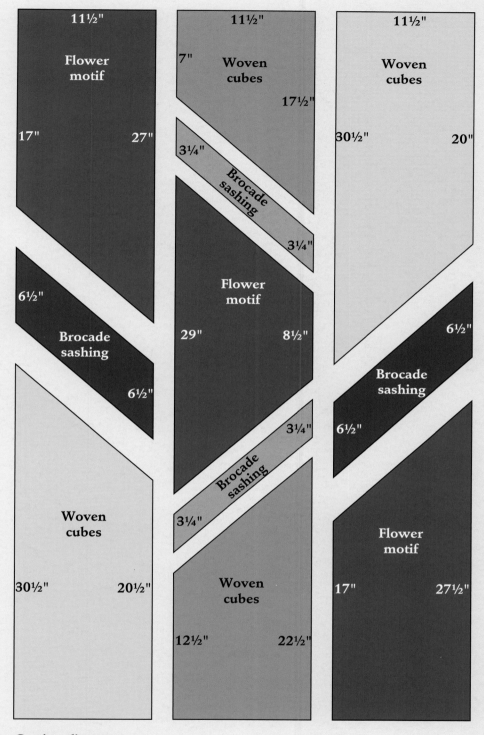

Cutting diagram

Note: Cut brocade silk sashing from the measurements shown here.

5. Stitch the underlined sections to the woven pieces. Press the seams toward the sashing.

6. Trim and butt the edges of 3 pieced panels together and stitch with narrow zigzag stitches as shown below.

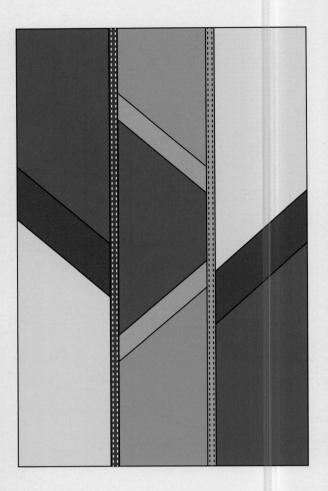

7. Cut 3 brocade strips 1¾" wide. Join with 45-degree seams, then cut two pieces 53" long. Fold under ⅜" lengthwise on both sides. Press. Cover the zigzag-stitched seams between three panels with the folded brocade strips and topstitch right next to folds.

8. Cut and apply the borders, see page 63.
2 strips 4½" x 34½" for the top and bottom borders
2 strips 4½" x 61" for the side borders

9. Add batting and backing to the quilt top. Quilt through all layers except in the woven sections.

10. Make 3-D flowers (pages 59–60).

For large 3-D flowers, cut 2" strips with silk dupioni and 1¾" strips with silk organza. Stitch two strips with right sides together using a ¼" seam allowance.

For small 3-D flowers, cut 1¾" strips with silk dupioni and 1½" strips with silk organza.

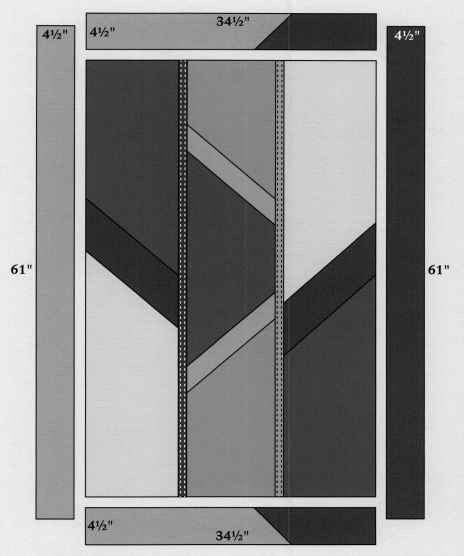

Applying borders

Stitch two strips with right sides together using a ¼" seam allowance

11. Make yo-yos for centers of the flowers.

12. Arrange flowers randomly across the surface of the quilt. Attach the flowers using crystal beads.

13. Cut 220" of 2½" binding strips for double-fold binding and apply to the quilt.

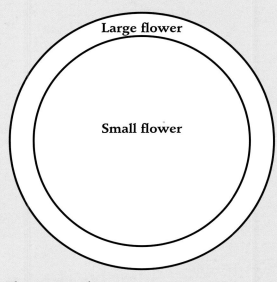

Flower templates

Weaving Gallery

SECRET GARDEN, art-to wear emsemble, made and modeled by the author

FLEURS DU PRINTEMPS, (SPRING FLOWERS), art-to-wear ensemble, made by the author

Rami Kim • Elegant • Cotton•Wool•Silk • Quilts   65

CUBES AND FLOWERS FEAST OF BLOSSOMS
art-to-wear ensemble, made by the author

KOREAN TRADITIONAL-STYLE ENSEMBLE
art-to-wear ensemble, made and modeled by the author

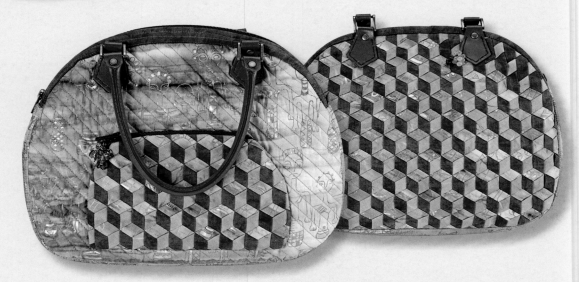

Leather bags with woven cube designs, made by the author

Bojahgey — Korean Wrapping Cloth

Bojahgey is a Korean wrapping cloth, one of many ancient Korean household items. It had been highly versatile from the use as practical covering cloths to protect foods from insects, as tote bags to hold and carry small items to the use as decorative wrappers for additional outer decoration of wedding and religious items.

Various types of fabrics from cottons to silks and designs were used in Bojahgey according to the owners' classes in past centuries.

Just as patchwork quilts in Western world, Bojahgey originally started as an effort to recycle old pieces of fabrics. However, as time passed, it developed into works of artistic harmony with full colors and shapes put together quite uniquely.

Rather than following certain sets of patterns, it is the characteristics of Bojahgey to emphasize free styles with less organized repetition to result in unplanned harmony.

Project 6
BOJAHGEY WITH TRIANGLE PATCHWORK
— COTTON QUILT
41" x 41", made by the author with designs and colors of 19th century

BOJAHGEY WITH TRIANGLE PATCHWORK

– COTTON QUILT

Yardage Requirements

- ⅜ yard EACH 15 assorted colored cottons (refer to the color chart, page 72)
- 7" x 9" Asian design brocade fabric swatch
- 1¼ yards backing
- 1¼ yards batting
- ⅜ yard binding

Cutting and Sewing Instructions

1. Cut 3 strips 3½" x 45" from EACH assorted color cotton. Using the triangle pattern provided cut out triangles as shown OR cut 3½" squares once on the diagonal. You need approximately 27 triangles of each color (400 triangles total).

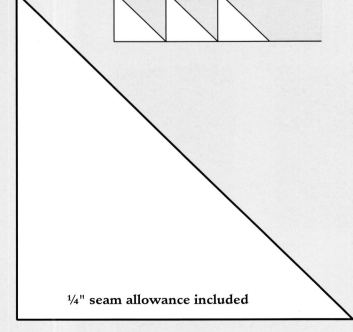

¼" **seam allowance included**

2. Selecting colors randomly or following the colors in the quilt photo, stitch diagonal seams of two different colored triangles to make a half-square triangle units (HSTs.) Shorten your stitch length to 2.0 and try not to stretch the seams while stitching the bias edges. Press all seams open.

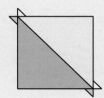

3. Trim off the bunny ears of the extended seam allowance.

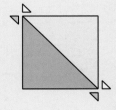

4. Start from row A at the bottom. Arrange 28 HSTs in 2 rows of 14 each as you please or follow the colors and values in the photo. Stitch 7 blocks of 4 HSTs each.

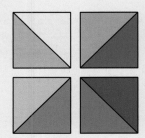
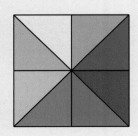

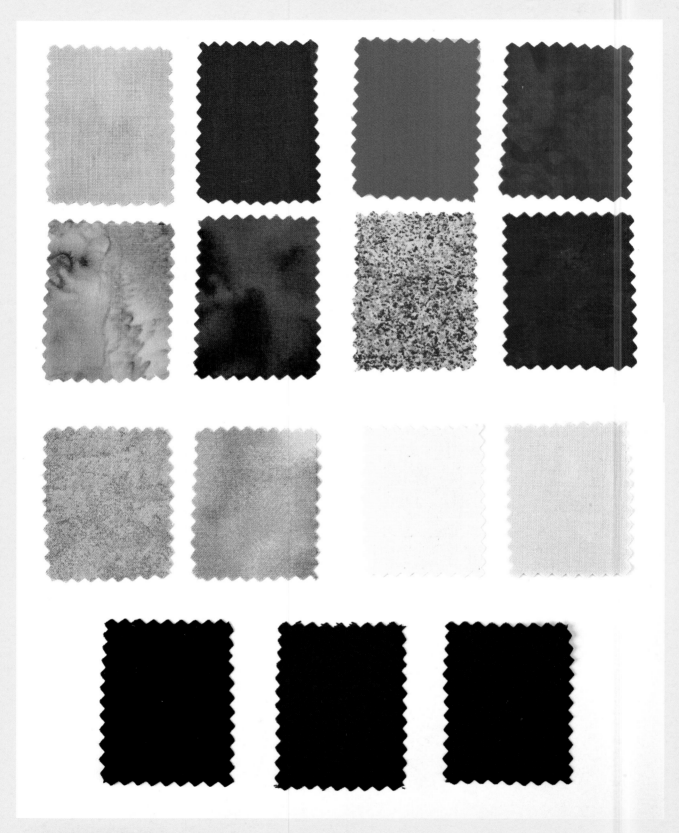

Bojahgey color chart

5. Connect 7 blocks together for row A. Press the seams open.

6. For row B, make 7 blocks and 1 half-block. Join with the half block at the right-hand end of the row.

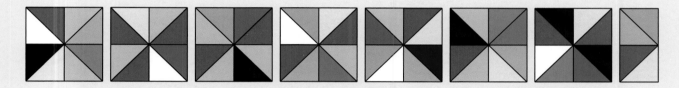

7. Place row B at the top edge of row A, offsetting it ¾" to the left. Join the two rows. Press the seams open. Trim off excess ends of row B to match the length of row A.

This deliberate offsetting reflects free-spirited styles of Bojahgey and non-matching seams adds animated movement of triangles.

8. For row C, make 7 blocks and 1 half block. Join with the half block at the left-hand end of the row.

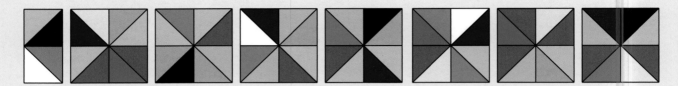

9. Place row C to the top edge of row B, offsetting 1½" to the left. Stitch together and trim off excess on both ends as shown.

trim   **trim**

1½"

10. For row D, make 6 blocks. Cut one insert of 7½" x 5⅝" of Asian-style brocade fabric. Add 3 blocks to both ends of the brocade insert.

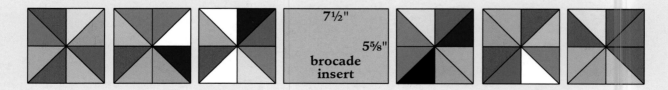

7½"

5⅝"

brocade insert

11. Place row D at the top edge of row C, centering the insert, and stitch. Trim off the excess on both ends.

trim   **trim**

center

12. For row E, repeat step 5, making and joining 7 blocks. (See step 5 figure, page 73.)

13. Place row E at the top edge of row D, centering it to the insert. Stitch.

14. For row F, repeat step 6, making and joining 7 blocks and 1 half block. (See step 6 figure, page 73.) Offset ¾" to the left when stitching row F to the top of row E. Trim off the excess.

15. For row G, repeat step 8, making and joining 7 blocks and 1 half block. (See step 8 figure, page 74.) Offset 1½" to the left and stitch to the top of row F. Trim off the excess.

16. Square the finished triangle patchworked piece to measure 36¼" x 36¼". This measurement might vary depending on individuals and machines. Measure your finished piece and decide the right size for you. Make sure to center the brocade insert on the finished piece.

17. Add borders following the diagram below, adjusting the measurements as needed to fit your piece. Make 4 HSTs for the four corners using the same size triangles in the quilt top. Insert different colors in borders as you wish.

18. Layer with batting and backing fabric and quilt through all three layers.

19. Prepare about 180" of double-fold binding by cutting and joining 2½" strips. Bind the edges.

Project 6 BOJAHGEY WITH TRIANGLE PATCHWORK

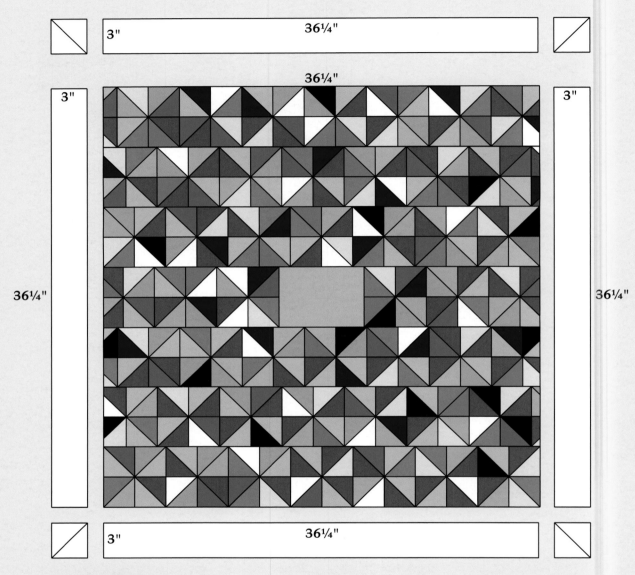

Quilt assembly

Bojahgey Gallery

Two more bojahgeys in Korean silks were made after my trip to Korea purchasing tons of scrumptious silks.

The first one is just like a summer quilt with no batting and seamed with French seams since stitches could be shown due to silk organza fabrics used.

SUMMER BOJAHGEY, 26" x 24½", made by the author

The second one is a one-layer patchworked piece with no batting or backing. Again, French seams were used. The silk brocade pieces in it were handed down from my husband's grandmother. They could easily be from 1900s and yet they still look beautiful.

Unlined Bojahgey, 29" x 35", made by the author

Meet Rami Kim

Rami Kim is a DNA scientist-turned fabric artist/quilter/instructor known nationally and internationally. She is a 17-time Best of Show winner, distinguished for her innovative art-to-wear.

Her passion is in contemporary art-to-wear, quilts, cloth dolls, and bags with special interest in three-dimensional textures. Rami is known for her own distinctive colors and techniques. Her first book, *Folded Fabric Elegance*, published by AQS (2007), is about her 3-D texturing techniques and new projects. Her second book, *Quilted Elegance*, also published by AQS (2009), focuses on reversible wearable arts, bags, and two-sided quilts.

Rami graduated from the University of California, San Francisco (UCSF), majoring in endocrinology. She worked at the Cancer Research Institute at UCSF before her passion and talent in fabric art drastically changed this biochemist's career years ago.

She says she'd rather spend even more time with beautiful fabrics and threads and beads than with DNA sequencing gels and radioactive isotopes of cold, gray science.

Check out her latest news and blog at www.ramikim.blogspot.com

more AQS Books

This is only a small selection of the books available from the American Quilter's Society. AQS books are known worldwide for timely topics, clear writing, beautiful color photos, and accurate illustrations and patterns. The following books are available from your local bookseller, quilt shop, or public library.

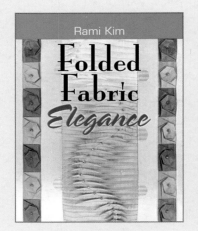

#7492

#8763

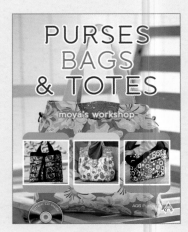

#8764

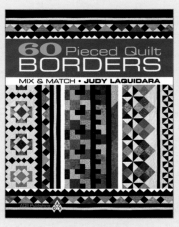

#8662

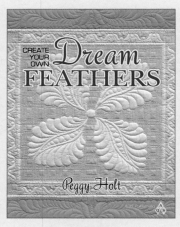

#8670

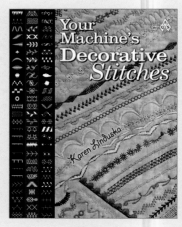

#8353

#8529

#8671

#8532

LOOK for these books nationally.
CALL or **VISIT** our website at

1-800-626-5420

www.AmericanQuilter.com